'Here is a wise and gentle introduc and practice for those who wonde discovery of the beauty of a worn . a pure morning light.'
Marilynne Robinson, author of *Gilead* and *Reading Genesis*

'Rowan Williams never disappoints. His subtle sensibility, profound understanding and luminous prose illuminates the deep and sometimes problematic aspects of Christianity. A book for believers and non-believers alike.'
Salley Vickers, author of *Miss Garnet's Angel* and *The Librarian*

'No one gets down to the beautiful essentials of faith like Rowan Williams. This is a compelling, wise and lucid invitation to explore the life-giving possibilities at the heart of the gospel. *Discovering Christianity* invites us to understand, maybe for the first time, why this particular and extraordinary story is worth building your life on.'
Sarah Bessey, author of *A Rhythm of Prayer* and *Field Notes for the Wilderness*

'This book is a gift for all those seeking to be brought back to – or invited into – the mysterious truth of the Christian faith. It manages the near-impossible task of being accessible yet profound; written with authority and warmth, clear-sightedness and wonder. It's a book I will be returning to again and again.'
Chine McDonald, author of *God is Not a White Man* and *Unmaking Mary*

'Stunning. Appropriately deep yet somehow also accessible, this is a wonderful place to start for the many people looking for a way into this strange old story.'
Elizabeth Oldfield, author of *Fully Alive: Tending to the Soul in Turbulent Times*

'Rowan Williams' *Discovering Christianity* made me feel like the Ethiopian eunuch in the Book of Acts – ready to go on my way rejoicing.'
Richard Coles, author of *Murder Before Evensong* and *The Madness of Grief*

'Rowan Williams offers a typically intelligent, attractive, and beguiling picture of what it means to be a Christian . . . When I read Williams I feel something coming to birth inside me; whispers from a shore I want to set out for.'
Mark Oakley, author of *The Splash of Words* and *My Sour Sweet Days*

DISCOVERING CHRISTIANITY

Born in 1950, **Rowan Williams** was educated in Swansea (Wales) and Cambridge. He studied for his theology doctorate in Oxford, after which he taught theology in a seminary near Leeds. From 1977 until 1986 he was engaged in academic and parish work in Cambridge, before returning to Oxford as Lady Margaret Professor of Divinity. In 1990 he became a Fellow of the British Academy. In 1992 Professor Williams became Bishop of Monmouth, and in 1999 he was elected as Archbishop of Wales. He became Archbishop of Canterbury in late 2002 with ten years' experience as a diocesan bishop and three as a primate in the Anglican Communion. As Archbishop, his main responsibilities were pastoral – whether leading his own diocese of Canterbury and the Church of England, or guiding the Anglican Communion worldwide. At the end of 2012, after ten years as Archbishop, he stepped down and moved to a new role as Master of Magdalene College, Cambridge. He retired in 2020 and is now living back in Wales.

Professor Williams is acknowledged internationally as an outstanding theological writer and teacher as well as an accomplished poet and translator. His interests include music, fiction and languages. His recent publications include *Being Human* (SPCK, 2019), *Luminaries* (SPCK, 2019) and *A Century of Poetry* (SPCK, 2022).

DISCOVERING CHRISTIANITY

A guide for the curious

Rowan Williams

First published in Great Britain in 2025

Chapters 1, 2 and 8 of this book contain text that was originally published in
What Is Christianity? A little book of guidance, published by SPCK in 2015.

SPCK
SPCK Group
Studio 101
The Record Hall
16–16A Baldwin's Gardens
London EC1N 7RJ
www.spck.org.uk

British Library Cataloguing-in-Publication Data
A catalogue record for this book is available from the British Library

ISBN 978–0–281–09064–8
eBook ISBN 978–0–281–09063–1

1 3 5 7 9 10 8 6 4 2

Typeset by Manila Typesetting Company
First printed in Great Britain by Clays Limited

eBook by Manila Typesetting Company

Produced on paper from sustainable sources

Contents

1
What is faith?

One of the great classics of Cambridge literature is Gwen Raverat's book *Period Piece: A Cambridge childhood*. In it she gives a picture of her family, and among her uncles and aunts are several figures of ripe eccentricity. One uncle was absolutely convinced that whenever he left the room the furniture would rearrange itself while he was out. He was constantly trying to get back quickly enough to catch it in the act. Now, that is admittedly a rather extreme case of Cambridge eccentricity, but I suspect that it may ring one or two bells with some readers. How many of us as children, I wonder, had a haunting suspicion that perhaps rooms rearranged themselves when we were out; that what we were seeing was not what continued to happen when our backs were turned?

I want to begin this chapter by thinking about that dimension of our human awareness that is persistently puzzled and frustrated, haunted by the idea that maybe what we see isn't the whole story, and that maybe our individual perception is not the measure of all truth. Our ordinary perceptions of the world around are often jolted by grief or joy. They're jolted in a way that leads us to want to say thank you, even if we don't know what or who to say thank you to. They're jolted when we don't know what to do with feelings for which we haven't yet got words or strategies. And that may be a long way from

Gwen Raverat's uncle, but something of the same idea is going on. What if the world is not as tame as I'm inclined to think it is? What if my perception of things (including my perception of the primacy of my individual needs or wants) is not the measure of everything? Religious feeling and perception is based on the sense of human limit, human vulnerability if you will. And it is based on the sense that to be human is not necessarily to be at the centre of things, or to be in control of things, as if I could have a kind of lighthouse vision that, circling about the entire scope of reality, lit up everything with an even light centred in me, my mind or my heart. But what if, after all, I'm not at the centre of everything, but part of a vast and rich interweaving of points of view and kinds of energy mingling and shaping one another?

There are two things we can do with this question – one of them healthy and one of them not so healthy; one of them leading to toxic religion and one of them leading to faith. Toxic religion results from using religious language, religious stories, as a way of pretending to ourselves that we are after all in charge, that actually we really are the centre of things and our limits can be overcome. We can come to believe we have access to absolute and infallible truth, to an even and just perspective on all things; we know what the world is really like and there's no more to be learned. It's the basis of toxic religion, but also of toxic forms of irreligious belief, especially when, even if a system calls itself atheistic, it still clings to certain religious ideas (bad ones) by pretending that human beings can actually answer all the questions they set themselves, and overcome all the limits that might threaten their power. And the trouble with bad religion – what makes it toxic – is that it's a way of teaching you to ignore what is real.

Seeing beyond the surface

What about the 'healthy' response, then? I'm going to suggest that one of the tests of actual faith, as opposed to bad religion, is whether it stops you ignoring things. Faith is most fully itself and most fully life-giving when it opens your eyes and uncovers for you a world larger than you ever thought – and, of course therefore, a world that can be a bit more alarming than you ever thought. The test of true faith is how much more it lets you see, and how much it stops you from denying, resisting or ignoring aspects of what is real.

I used to know a very remarkable man who was, for twenty-six years, a senior consultant psychiatrist in Broadmoor Hospital – an incredibly testing job. He was also a great Shakespearean enthusiast, and one of his favourite lines was from *The Tempest*, where Prospero says to Miranda, 'What seest thou else?' That, he said, was the question that kept him going as a psychiatrist. Confronted with horrendous and tragic situations, with people deeply disturbed and locked up in their own fantasies, he would have to ask himself repeatedly, '"What seest thou else?" What more is there to see?' And for him, the enterprise of religious faith was about this seeing more – seeing that the world can't be fully seen just by one pair of eyes, or even by the sum total of all pairs of human eyes, and seeing that the world has a dimension of real strangeness, a depth not sounded.

Faith is most fully itself and most fully life-giving when it opens your eyes and uncovers for you a world larger than you ever thought.

This is where religious faith most overlaps with art, but also with creative science. Creative science, remember, begins in the conviction that there is something not seen, there is something that I or we have been ignoring and it's time we stopped ignoring it. And the arts – poetry, sculpture, painting, drama – are all rooted in this feeling that the world is more than it shows to any one person in any one image at any one moment.

Religious faith, in other words, is a process of educating our vision and our passions. Educating our vision so that we understand how to see what we don't yet fully see; to see behind surfaces, the depth that we're not going to master. And educating our passions in the sense of helping ourselves to grow up 'humanly' in such a way that we don't take fright at this strangeness and mysteriousness and run for all we're worth.

Faith causes us to inhabit a larger world. One of the problems of perception in our world today is that it so often looks as though faith leads you into a smaller world and makes smaller human beings. Whereas those of us who try to live with and in it would want to say that actually it's an immeasurably larger world. There's a famous sixteenth-century woodcut that you sometimes see reproduced in history books, which shows a human figure pushing its head through the firmament of heaven – the smooth, tidy firmament of heaven with the little stars on it. This person has pushed through it and is suddenly looking up into a sky that they've never seen before, packed with strange stars. That woodcut is often taken as a kind of image of what it felt like in the sixteenth century as the Renaissance unfolded, and people realised that the world was immeasurably bigger than they'd ever thought. It's quite often used as an image of resistance to traditional Christianity and religious authority. Yet I want to say that it ought to be an image of authentic faith, of a real understanding of what the tradition of religious practice does for you, pushing you through the smooth painted surface, out towards a sky with stars you've never seen.

The light of the gospel

How does this play out specifically in the context of Christian faith? And why might that be worth taking seriously?

At this point I'm going to stop talking anything resembling philosophy for a bit and turn to the Gospel according to John, and in particular to the story of how Jesus healed a blind man, found in John chapter 9. It's worth quoting this at length:

> As he walked along, he saw a man blind from birth. His disciples asked him, 'Rabbi, who sinned, this man or his parents, that he was born blind?' Jesus answered, 'Neither this man nor his parents sinned; he was born blind so that God's works might be revealed in him. We must work the works of him who sent me while it is day; night is coming, when no one can work. As long as I am in the world, I am the light of the world.' When he had said this, he spat on the ground and made mud with the saliva and spread the mud on

the man's eyes, saying to him, 'Go, wash in the pool of Siloam' (which means Sent). Then he went and washed and came back able to see. The neighbours and those who had seen him before as a beggar began to ask, 'Is this not the man who used to sit and beg?' Some were saying, 'It is he'. Others were saying, 'No, but it is someone like him'. He kept saying, 'I am he'. But they kept asking him, 'Then how were your eyes opened?' He answered, 'The man called Jesus made mud, spread it on my eyes, and said to me, "Go to Siloam and wash". Then I went and washed and received my sight.' They said to him, 'Where is he?' He said, 'I do not know'.

They brought to the Pharisees the man who had formerly been blind. Now it was a Sabbath day when Jesus made the mud and opened his eyes. Then the Pharisees also began to ask him how he had received his sight. He said to them, 'He put mud on my eyes. Then I washed, and now I see.' Some of the Pharisees said, 'This man is not from God, for he does not observe the Sabbath'. Others said, 'How can a man who is a sinner perform such signs?' And they were divided. So they said again to the blind man, 'What do you say about him? It was your eyes he opened.' He said, 'He is a prophet'.

The Jews did not believe that he had been blind and had received his sight until they called the parents of the man who had received his sight and asked them, 'Is this your son, who you say was born blind? How then does he now see?' His parents answered, 'We know that this is our son and that he was born blind, but we do not know how it is that now he sees, nor do we know who opened his eyes. Ask him; he is of age. He will speak for himself.' His parents said this because they were afraid of the Jews, for the Jews had already agreed that anyone who confessed Jesus to be the Messiah would be put out of the synagogue. Therefore his parents said, 'He is of age; ask him'.

So for the second time they called the man who had been blind, and they said to him, 'Give glory to God! We know that this man is a sinner.' He answered, 'I do not know whether he is a sinner. One thing I do know, that though I was blind, now I see.' They said to him, 'What did he do to you? How did he open your eyes?' He answered them, 'I have told you already, and you would not listen. Why do you want to hear it again? Do you also want to become his disciples?' Then they reviled him, saying, 'You are his disciple, but we are disciples of Moses. We know that God has spoken to Moses, but as for this man, we do not know where he comes from.' The man answered, 'Here is an astonishing thing! You do not know where he comes from, yet he opened my eyes. We know that God does not listen to sinners, but he does listen to one who worships him and obeys his will. Never since the world began has it been heard that anyone opened the eyes of a person born blind. If this man were not from God, he could do nothing.' They answered him, 'You were born entirely in sins, and are you trying to teach us?' And they drove him out.

Jesus heard that they had driven him out, and when he found him he said, 'Do you believe in the Son of Man?' He answered, 'And who is he, sir? Tell me, so that I may believe in him.' Jesus said to him, 'You have seen him, and the one speaking with you is he'. He said, 'Lord, I believe'. And he worshipped him. Jesus said, 'I came into this world for judgement, so that those who do not see may see and those who do see may become blind'. Some of the Pharisees who were with him heard this and said to him, 'Surely we are not blind, are we?' Jesus said to them, 'If you were blind, you would not have sin. But now that you say, "We see", your sin remains.' (John 9:1–41)

I can't think of anywhere better to start in trying to spell out a little bit of what the Christian story of seeing looks and feels like. Notice how at the end of the story Jesus says to the hostile experts who challenge him, 'But now that you say, "We see", your sin remains.' Or as it might be translated, 'Because you say you can see, you're stuck in your alienation from the full truth.' In other words, 'Only if you recognise that you can't see can you find your way.' It's one of those many startling paradoxes that occur so often in John's Gospel. Jesus is addressing the religious experts of the day and effectively saying, 'Your problem is that you can't see that you can't see. You can't see what it is that your habits, your status and your skill prevent you from engaging with.'

As the gospel story unfolds, we get a clearer picture of exactly what it is that these experts can't see. They can't see the mechanisms that drive them: mechanisms that lead them to be deeply afraid; mechanisms that allow them to use violence to protect their safe and self-justified positions; mechanisms that allow scapegoating, which seek security at the expense of others. They can't see all of that noisy, mechanical stuff going on inside them and so, says Jesus, they are stuck in their self-destructive habits. They don't know they can't see, and when vision is offered to them, they run from it.

Well, that's not entirely surprising. Most of us, when candid friends or even more candid enemies offer us pictures of what we might really be like, are inclined to run. Very few human beings, whatever we may like to tell ourselves, have a natural taste for hearing the truth about themselves. When somebody says to us, 'Do you really want to know what I think?' the honest answer in most cases would be, 'Actually, no.'

So far, so obvious, you might say, and you might feel you don't entirely blame the religious experts in the gospel story for panicking at the prospect of being shown the mechanisms of their own fear and violence.

But what makes the difference in John's Gospel is that the story not only portrays a vision of ourselves as failing, ignorant and frightened. The story of Jesus, as John tells it, also involves a vision of something else, which he calls glory: the radiance and the beauty that are at the root of everything. In the light of that radiance, we can't keep up the pretence of self-justification and self-protection. In the full light of that radiance, we can't be like the religious experts and say, 'I see, I've got it,' and put the experience and

Very few human beings, whatever we may like to tell ourselves, have a natural taste for hearing the truth about themselves.

the knowledge in a package in our pocket. Jesus' mission in this Gospel is described very clearly as the process of bringing that radical, radiant beauty to light in this world in such a way that only the most resolutely self-justifying and the most terminally terrified will want to resist.

Self-justification, fear and violence, and all the rest of the package, become impossible in the light of that radiance, because according to the gospel the radiance itself is the presence of an utter unselfishness at the heart of everything. What lies behind and beneath all reality, the gospel says, is an action whereby the most full, powerful, resourceful reality we can imagine lets go of itself, and makes over its own fullness of joy and life so that there may be life in another.

It begins in eternity; it fleshes itself out time and again in the world's history. The radiant beauty – the glory – of that gospel is the glory of a divine letting go, and faced with that we're delivered, so we hope and pray, from the prison of violent self-justification. Why? Because if we are faced with that vision of an endless, unlimited unselfishness, there is no one we have to persuade, cajole or manipulate to love us; there is no hostile, defensive, cosmic tyrant somewhere over there that we have to placate.

All we have is an endless gift of unconditional love. All we have is what again in John's Gospel we see referred to as an unceasing work, an unceasing labour of giving life. At one point in the Gospel Jesus is defending the fact that he might technically be breaking the Sabbath by healing somebody, and he says, 'My Father is still at work, and I am still at work.' There can be no interruption of this unselfish act of life-giving, healing restoration and affirmation.

We can perhaps recognise what a wonderful truth that would be, if it were indeed true. And we might wonder how, precisely, such a vision could come to feel natural or possible for us. But that's where the story of Jesus winds the tension more and more tightly. As the story unfolds, we begin to see more clearly just how securely we are locked into our self-deceptions. Gradually, as the story goes on, we see more and more deeply how and why human beings want to resist that double vision: the true vision of their own fear and the true vision of the love that overcomes it. And it seems in the story as though fear wins. Jesus is condemned and executed. The human refusal to see finally means his death on the cross. But, says the gospel, that death is itself a moment of glory yet again. Because there we see what a complete letting go of the self in love actually looks like.

The symbol is lifted up before us, the symbol of a love with no conditions and no defences. The cross is itself glory. The death of Jesus shows what is indestructible in the love of God, and the work goes on. God does not stop working, does not stop being this unselfish God because of our refusals. And so unbroken is that work, it goes on through and beyond the death of Jesus on the cross; life breaks through once more. What is alive in Jesus cannot be suppressed by death, and returns actively loving and inviting as always.

Almost infinitely more could be said about the Gospel of John, one of the most inexhaustible texts in the whole of the Bible, but I hope I've said enough to show how much of it talks about faith as seeing. It is about that double vision of myself as frightened and potentially violent, and of

God as radiant, consistent and unceasingly creative. And that's what we're invited into. We're invited into Christian faith, recognising the self-deception, recognising the glory. Indeed, in recognising the glory – the radiance of an unceasing, selfless love – we are somehow enabled to face more courageously and more fully our own self-deceit.

The first two things that Jesus says in John's Gospel are, 'What do you want?' and, 'Come and see.' There couldn't really be a better introduction to faith. What do you want? Do you actually want to change your life? Do you actually want human wholeness? If you do, come and see. So the gospel story begins not with an argument, but with an invitation to examine yourself and be in a place where you can see something different: 'What seest thou else?'

We're invited to take time with this story, because its claim, although fairly simple, is quite a devastating one. The claim that John's Gospel makes, indeed the whole of the Christian tradition makes, is that there is a single moment in the history of the human world where that world is completely transparent to the love that made it, where glory appears in a human face.

2

What is Christianity?

Imagine someone watching, over a period of about one year, the things that happen in a Christian church. They would be aware that one day of the week has special significance. And if they are observing what happens in a historically Christian country, they would notice that Sunday is seen as important for meeting and praying. They would see that Christians meet to sing and speak to a God whom they describe as the maker of all things and the judge of all things, and that they kneel or bow in the presence of this God, thanking him and acknowledging their failures and sinfulness. They would see that extracts from a holy book are read in public and that instruction is given by leaders of the congregation in how to understand this book. They would perhaps notice that most of the prayers end with words referring to someone called Jesus Christ, and describing him as 'Lord'.

They would see that at different seasons Christians celebrate the birth of Jesus and also commemorate his death and his miraculous return from death. Sometimes they would hear prayers and blessings mentioning 'the Father, the Son and the Holy Spirit'. And finally, they would see that new members are brought into the community by a ceremony of pouring water on them or immersing them in water, and that the most regular action performed by communities of different kinds is the blessing and sharing of bread and wine. They would notice, perhaps with bewilderment or even shock, that this sharing of bread and wine is described as sharing the body and blood of Jesus. They would (I hope) see that the language used about human beings living together in 'communion' and about the making of women and men 'in God's image' has a clear impact on how believing communities think about and respond to the realities of injustice, exclusion, prejudice and violence; how they engage with those who are treated as dispensable by their societies.

In this chapter, I am trying to think about what questions might arise for someone looking at Christians from the outside in the way I have just imagined. This chapter is in fact based on a talk composed for a non-European Muslim audience, trying not to use too much 'insider' language. These may or may not be the questions you have. But perhaps the attempt to answer these questions will help bring other questions more clearly into focus.

God: Father, Son and Holy Spirit

Let me begin with the most obvious features of Christian prayer. Christians pray 'through Jesus Christ our Lord'. And the best known of all Christian prayers begins with the words 'Our Father in heaven'. These belong together. Probably the most important Christian belief is that people are given the right to speak to God in exactly the same way that Jesus did, because the life, the power, the Spirit that filled Jesus is given to us also.

Probably the most important Christian belief is that people are given the right to speak to God in exactly the same way that Jesus did, because the life, the power, the Spirit that filled Jesus is given to us also.

Christians believe that Jesus, son of Mary, is fully a human being. But Christians believe more than that. Because of the divine authority that he shows in his power to teach and to forgive, as the Gospels describe it, Christians say also that the whole of his human life is the direct effect of God's action working in him at every moment. The image used by some Christian thinkers is that his human life is like iron that has been heated in the fire until it has the same power to burn as the fire does.

Christians call Jesus the Son of God. But they do not mean by this that God is physically his father, or that he is made to be another God alongside the one God. Christians say rather that the one God is alive and real in three eternal and distinct ways. God is first the source of everything, the life from which everything flows out. But then Christians say that this one God is also living and real in that 'flowing out'. The life that comes from him is not something different from him. It reflects all that he is. It shows his glory and beauty, and communicates them. Christians say that God has a perfect and eternal image of his glory, sometimes called his wisdom, sometimes called his word (originally meaning not simply 'speech' but something more like 'mind' or 'intelligence that communicates'), sometimes called his son, though this is never to be understood in a physical and literal way. And Christians say that the one God, who is both source and outward-flowing life, who is both Father and Son, is also active as the sheer energy of the love that the Father gives the Son and the Son gives back to the Father. So he is active in the word as the power that draws everything back to God, leading and guiding human beings – and indeed the whole universe – towards unity with the wisdom and goodness of God. This is the power Christians call Holy Spirit.

So when Christians speak of the Father, the Son and the Holy Spirit, they do not at all mean to say that there are three gods – as if there were three divine people in heaven, like three human people in a room. Certainly Christians believe that the three ways in which God eternally exists and acts are distinct from one another, and they talk about the three 'persons' that make up the life of God; but it is a mistake to think they are distinct in the way that things in the world or even individuals in the world are distinct, as if they were stand-alone divine objects.

Turning to what Christians believe about Jesus, perhaps we can see why they say that he is the Son of God. Because the eternal word and wisdom of God completely occupy his human mind and body, Christians say that in him this word and wisdom has 'become flesh' – has been 'incarnated', to use the technical Christian term. Just as the word and wisdom eternally reflects God's glory and beauty, so in our human world, in human history, Jesus reflects this glory and beauty, showing us both the splendour of divine love and the true dignity and glory of humanity as God intends it to be. Because the word and wisdom of God is sometimes described in the Jewish Scriptures of the Old Testament as a child of God – and also because these Scriptures often call the kings of God's people who rule according to wisdom the sons of God – Christians have come to say that Jesus, who embodies God's wisdom and is anointed as ruler of God's people, is God's Son. And, as we have seen, from the very

start Christian thinkers have said that this language must
not be thought of in any physical way.

When Jesus himself prays to God in his own human
voice, he calls him Father. And what we must now add to
what we have said so far is that this title expresses not only
acknowledgement on the part of Jesus that his whole being
comes directly from God, but also the trust and complete
confidence that he enjoys with God. As the Gospel of John
tells us over and over again, Jesus knows the very mind and
heart of God and can reveal it completely and authoritatively
to those he calls to be with him. When Christians pray in
the name of Jesus and say 'Our Father', they are saying to
God: 'You have promised that when I pray, you will hear the
voice of Jesus, and you will look upon me with the same love
that Jesus knew.' When Christians pray, they stand in the
place of Jesus. They speak his words, hoping in confidence
that they will receive the love he receives from the one he
calls Father.

Jesus: the human face of God

Many who are not Christian think that this confidence in
Jesus means Christians rely upon Jesus instead of trying
to obey God's commands for themselves. Other faiths
sometimes criticise Christians for treating human beings as
if they were not fully responsible for their actions. But the
Christian belief is this. When God created the world, he
made all things according to his will. But the first human
beings refused to obey God, although they knew what was
asked of them and what was offered them. By this refusal,

they started a process of corruption in the world which has spread to everyone born into it. Even before a newborn child has learned to speak, it will have been touched and affected by a climate of alienation from God. We are all deeply affected by the actions of others, and sometimes we find that the results of other people's actions make it hard or even impossible to do what is right. Christians say that this is something that to some extent limits the freedom of every human being. The purpose of God is there and it is plain enough in itself, but we are held in prison by this history of refusing and ignoring God. Such is the teaching of St Paul. This is what Christians mean when they sometimes speak of 'original sin' – the confusion and betrayal of God's purpose that is there in our world even before we have done anything.

Only God the Creator can restore the freedom to live in a way that is in harmony with his will and his nature. How does he do this? When he brings the human life of Jesus into being in the womb of Mary, he brings into being a life that will be perfectly in harmony with who and what God is, because it is a human life completely filled with divine life – with the creative love and endless resourcefulness of God's own being. Jesus thus shows us what a human life is like when it is lived as it should be. But he does more than just show us. Because of his own perfect harmony with God's will and goodness, he is able to offer himself to rejection and death, so that by his death there may be a restored relationship of love between God and humanity. Christians say that Jesus, as he goes to the cross, accepts all the suffering that is the consequence for human beings of their rebellion and weakness. He pays the price of human betrayal and weakness. Because he accepts this suffering as an act of love, he changes what is possible for human beings. They need no longer despair that they can never love God or respond fittingly to God. The death and rising again of Jesus somehow releases into the world the divine breath of life – that transforming energy of love that we call the Holy Spirit. And those who commit to living in the company of Jesus are those in whom that release of the unprecedented power of divine love is supposed to be most clearly witnessed.

Christians believe that when they come in trust to Jesus and identify with him – when they stand in his place and speak with his words – the Holy Spirit is giving them the freedom to live according to God's will, reflecting God's own character. Once they were not free, because the only kind of human fellowship or togetherness possible was togetherness in an inheritance of disharmony and betrayal that affects us all. But Jesus creates a new kind of fellowship, a relationship with himself that is going to be stronger than the deep currents that pull people towards destructive and self-serving behaviour. Paul says that this means there is a new creation. We are able to start over again, and to show in our community life what humanity looks like when it is rescued from competitive selfishness and mutual fear.

Christians have always found it hard to say exactly how this works. Some speak of Jesus taking the punishment for sin in our place; some speak of him offering himself as a sacrifice. Some speak of him winning a victory over Satan and setting prisoners free. It seems that there is no one way of saying this correctly. But what matters is this. In the life of Jesus, the completeness of divine love breaks into a world

Christians believe that when they come in trust to Jesus and identify with him – when they stand in his place and speak with his words – the Holy Spirit is giving them the freedom to live according to God's will, reflecting God's own character.

in which human beings are not free and not in contact with that love. By approaching his death as an act of love for human beings, by speaking about it (as he does in the Gospels) as a sort of payment to the powers of evil that will release people from the effects of the sin of the first human beings, Jesus 'opens the kingdom of heaven to all believers', to use the words of an ancient Christian hymn.

And because God brings Jesus back from death to meet again with his followers, Christians know that his life is not a thing of the past. He is still alive, eternally alive. He calls people to be with him just as he did during his life on earth. And so day by day he creates that community of fellowship with him that gives human beings the possibility of living differently, in harmony with God. In the words of John's Gospel, he 'breathes' into his followers the power of the Holy Spirit, so that they are drawn back to God and his ways. Because he rose from death 'on the first day of the week', according to the Gospels, Sunday has always been a special day for Christians. And the Easter season is the greatest of all Christian festivals.

When Christians receive the Holy Spirit, they still have to use their freedom to choose what is good and to work with all their powers of mind and body to show the world what God's purpose is for human beings in community, living with honesty, fairness and compassion. But in fellowship with Jesus, Christians know that they have the help of the Spirit, giving them strength to resist temptation, and wisdom to see where it lies. Christians also know that when they fail or fall back, as sometimes they are bound to do, the forgiving love of God will give them another opportunity to serve him, to try to model their lives on the life of Jesus and to let the freedom and love that he has planted in their hearts change all that they do and say.

3

What is theology?

We'll start with a passage from the Acts of the Apostles, the story of the very beginning of the Christian community in Jerusalem, the day of Pentecost.

> When the day of Pentecost had come, they were all together in one place. And suddenly from heaven there came a sound like the rush of a violent wind, and it filled the entire house where they were sitting. Divided tongues, as of fire, appeared among them, and a tongue rested on each of them. All of them were filled with the Holy Spirit and began to speak in other languages, as the Spirit gave them ability. (Acts 2:1–4)

What was the reaction? People were amazed and perplexed. They asked one another, 'What does this mean?' or, as the original Greek might be translated, 'What on earth is this about?' And of course the reaction of the cynics was that the apostles had been on the bottle all night.

What was going on? Some new kind of human experience, of human togetherness, had suddenly erupted into the world. It was a kind of human experience, a kind of togetherness, that allowed people to speak to strangers in their own language. Whatever exactly that means, whatever exactly went on during that first day of Pentecost, that's what people remembered: suddenly insiders were able to speak to outsiders, suddenly barriers dropped with a great crash. Something new, some new kind of connectedness, had taken place.

What was that about? You can't just say, 'That was amazing!' and leave it at that. You're a human being, so you've got a mind. You need to think about it, you need to talk about it. So on the day of Pentecost, Peter, one of Jesus' close followers, gets up and talks about it; he is, you could say, doing his first bit of theology. 'What's going on? Let me tell you; let me make some connections for you.' He explains how the visions in Hebrew Scripture of an outpouring of the breath of the Lord into the life and words of his people will one day come true in such a way that this outpouring becomes universal. Peter sets out to tell a story and make some connections so as to explain what is going on.

There's another side to this, of course, which is that if nothing much is going on, nothing much will happen theologically. Theology overflows – bursts out in flood – when there's a lot going on. Which is why in the very first ages of the Christian Church there's a lot of theology – and sometimes it can look fairly confusing. But this is because so much is happening: people are aware that their universe is expanding all the time, that there are more things to come to terms with, more connections to make. So the theology we find in Christian Scripture, and indeed in quite a lot of the writing of the first few hundred years of Christianity, isn't set out in nice orderly bullet points in a sort of PowerPoint presentation. It's more a matter of many people scratching their heads and talking intently and often argumentatively to each other, and saying, 'Does that

Theology overflows – bursts out in flood – when there's a lot going on. Which is why in the very first ages of the Christian Church there's a lot of theology – and sometimes it can look fairly confusing.

make sense?' Thinking for a moment that they've got it and then realising they haven't and will have to start again.

That's very much how St Paul writes, for example. It's always worth remembering that Paul didn't know he was writing the New Testament. He was certainly inspired by the Spirit of God in his writing, but he didn't pick up his pen or start dictating to his assistant thinking, 'I've got to write a chapter of the New Testament today.' He sat down, he prayed, he thought and he scribbled or dictated at speed. Some of what resulted is wonderfully clear, poetic, profound. And some just reflects effort and puzzlement, and occasionally the reader has the sense that he is in danger of just digging the hole a bit deeper. There is a famous passage in his first letter to the church in Corinth, where he's writing about why women should cover their heads in churches. After a long and rather convoluted argument, he simply concludes by saying, almost with exasperation, 'Well, we simply don't do it,' and then moves on rapidly to another subject. This is so often what theology looks like as it takes shape: questions are raised and the answers don't line up neatly. But it is all still part of that task of trying to come to terms with what's happening. If what was happening had not been diffuse and rich, baffling and exhilarating, nothing would have been said.

Here is another episode from the Acts of the Apostles, this very early record of how the Church spread in the communities around the eastern Mediterranean. It's at the beginning of the nineteenth chapter:

Paul passed through the interior regions and came to Ephesus, where he found some disciples. He said to them, 'Did you receive the Holy Spirit when you became believers?' They replied, 'No, we have not even heard that there is a Holy Spirit'. Then he said, 'Into what, then, were you baptized?' They answered, 'Into John's baptism'. Paul said, 'John baptized with the baptism of repentance, telling the people to believe in the one who was to come after him, that is, in Jesus'. On hearing this, they were baptized in the name of the Lord Jesus. When Paul had laid his hands on them, the Holy Spirit came upon them, and they spoke in tongues and prophesied. (Acts 19:1–6)

It sounds as though Paul has noticed that not much is going on with these people. They have received some form of baptism – apparently something like the ritual washing that had been practised by John the Baptist in the gospel stories, a solemn acknowledgement of sins and failures, and a commitment to try to start again. They've acknowledged their need for forgiveness and have brought their lives before God in the hope of turning them around. But what else ('What seest thou else?')? Nothing much is happening in them yet that looks like radical change; they're not yet being transformed by the Holy Spirit. And it's when this starts happening, when they and their world seem to be changing in ways beyond their grasp, that they need the new words, the language of the Holy Spirit. Paul comes along and says, 'Something is going to happen, something so radical that you are going to need to talk about the Holy Spirit from this point on.'

Making new connections

So the first theological question is: 'What on earth is going on?' Theology comes out of that, as new connections are made and the enormous new map of the world begins to acquire a bit of shape and detail. Transformation is, I think, the key to how theology works in the New Testament. Things change, horizons expand, and it's not surprising that Paul talks about being a new creation. When anybody comes alive in Jesus Christ, it's as if creation has begun all over again. Coming to terms with, and finding words for, the nature and scale of that change is what Paul is constantly trying to do.

You can see how the connections begin to be made, and it's possible to have some sense of the kind of changes that people were grappling with. The first Christians were, it seems, overcome by, swept away with, a new kind of praying, a new way of talking to God. Paul in his letters says that the heart of this is being able to call God Father. We can have an intimate family relationship with God that nothing has really prepared us for. Beneath and behind all the outpourings of prayer and praise is this basic discovery about how we should see and experience our relationship with the divine. So when Paul tries to define what the essence of the life of the Spirit is, it is this that he constantly returns to.

But how does this change happen? It happens in connection with the life and death and rising from death of Jesus of Nazareth – a man roughly Paul's own age, perhaps a few years older; a man well within the living memory of people around; and a man who somehow managed to make the entire universe look different. Part of that difference is that for those who listened to him he opened up a new way of relating to God as Father.

And that is a challenging enough start. Not every travelling rabbi and wonder-worker changes the way you see the universe. It seems that you have to find something a little bit more to say about Jesus of Nazareth than that he was a rather remarkable person and it's a pity he's not with us any longer. But how much more can you say, and where are you going to find the raw materials for it? This is where Paul starts pushing the boundaries and making new connections, like all the writers of the New Testament. The newness, the transformation, the new universe, is connected mysteriously with what went on around Jesus. And this includes the events around his execution and what followed, the profoundly confusing set of encounters that persuaded Jesus' closest friends that he was no longer dead and never would be. It was not just the fact that Jesus was as an individual raised to life again, but somehow when he began to live again, new life flooded the entire world.

That flooding of the entire world is what is described by Paul and others as the work of the divine Spirit; what Jesus' life and death and resurrection mean is inseparable from the arrival of the Spirit. But if this Spirit is genuinely the Spirit of God, the questions around Jesus become more complex still. Here is a human being who is somehow letting loose the very breath of God's life into the world. Say what you like about him, but it is difficult to class him as merely an interesting dead person who lived long ago.

Here is Paul pushing away at these boundaries as he writes at the beginning of the first letter to Corinth: 'We proclaim

Christ crucified, a stumbling-block to Jews and foolishness to gentiles, but to those who are the called, both Jews and Greeks, Christ the power of God and the wisdom of God' (1 Corinthians 1:23–4).

And in the second letter to Corinth, he writes about the glory of Jesus: 'Indeed, what once had glory has in this respect lost its glory because of the greater glory, for if what was set aside came through glory, much more has the permanent come in glory!' (2 Corinthians 3:10–11).

And he moves from there into the great image in 2 Corinthians 4: 'For it is the God who said, "Light will shine out of darkness", who has shone in our hearts to give the light of the knowledge of the glory of God in the face of Christ' (verse 6).

All this is saying that in Jesus the glory, the overwhelming radiance, of God is displayed. And not just displayed. It is somehow completely and lastingly at home in him; it lives in him. Turn forward from here to the later letters to the Ephesians and the Colossians and the boundaries are being pushed still further. If this is a human being in whom the glory of God actually lives habitually – if when you look at Jesus you look at a man so connected with God that you can't drive a wedge between what he does and what God does – this means that a man who is roughly Paul's own age and died within his memory was the embodiment and conduit of the love that created the world. And so, because he is associated with the beginning of everything, he is associated with the new beginning – the new creation – in the lives of all those who trust in him and try to stay in his company. It's as if Paul is making the strongest possible connection between what changes in a person's life as a result of trusting Jesus and the literally unimaginable change that is something emerging from nothing. The new creation, the new horizon in the life that faith brings, is connected through Jesus with the very beginning of all things – when God simply declared that something should exist that was not God, so it might live in joy and beauty by sharing the love God eternally pours out.

This is the essence of theology: making connections at this level of adventurous imagination. It tries to answer the question of what on earth is going on as faith comes alive, by exploring more and more of the resonances of the central story. Some books about theology may give you the impression that, for the first three or four hundred years of the Church's life, what was going on was that a lot of people with rather too much time on their hands were simply making up a lot of complicated theories about Jesus. They were developing ever more abstract patterns and more and more technical language about him. It leads some to say that what we need is to get back to the simple language of the Bible. But the awkward truth is that the simple language of the Bible is very seldom as simple as some people would like it to be, and it will always push you into asking more and more big questions. You can't just freeze the film and say, 'That's enough thinking.' It is not as if this is thinking for its own sake – idle theorising. This is why it is better to talk about theology as the process of making sense of Christianity. When you try to make sense of life, it's not just a matter of theory. It's finding a picture of your life and your world that you can live with; a sense of where you belong and how. So it is with the theological enterprise:

The awkward truth is that the simple language of the Bible is very seldom as simple as some people would like it to be, and it will always push you into asking more and more big questions.

it is not just theory or speculation, but a discovery of what and where you might be in the light of a new framework of experience. The simple language of Scripture, after all, includes not only Paul's more complicated riffs on various themes. It also includes the truly extraordinary beginning of John's Gospel – that slow almost stately unfolding of the connection between the beginning of everything and the beginning of new life in Christ:

> In the beginning was the Word, and the Word was with God, and the Word was God. He was in the beginning with God. All things came into being through him, and without him not one thing came into being. What has come into being in him was life, and the life was the light of all people. The light shines in the darkness, and the darkness did not overcome it. (John 1:1–5)

Then a few verses later: 'And the Word became flesh and lived among us, and we have seen his glory, the glory as of a father's only son, full of grace and truth' (John 1:14). This wonderfully calm, eloquent exposition, immense truths in brief words, is precisely where Paul's extravagant metaphors and similes lead us. It brings us to the recognition that when we look at Jesus, we look at that energy in which the whole world holds together, and through which the breath of God is breathed into us if we are ready to do more than just look, and open our hearts to receive.

This is the point of theology.

4
Why church?

We saw in the last chapter how theology gets its initial impetus, for a Christian, in the pressure to think more deeply about how and why Jesus and the Spirit are connected, with a radically fresh sense of who and what human beings are. And this is why, of course, one of the central issues in theology has always been and no doubt will always be the doctrine of the Holy Trinity: God the Father, God the Son, God the Holy Spirit. The new world into which Christians are introduced is a world where we call God Father because of Jesus and understand this as the effect of God's own Spirit breathing into us. And this is why the doctrine of the Holy Trinity is not just something locked up in textbooks, a technical affair that only theological anoraks would want to explore. For Christians it's about who we are and where we live. Christians see themselves as living in the middle of this mystery, in the middle of the Father and the Son and the Holy Spirit. And Christian theology is about finding where we are in that great unfolding of divine life around us – the outpouring of the Father's love, the adoration that the Son gives to the Father, the breathing out of the Spirit to fill the whole creation. It's all about finding where we really and lastingly live.

Of course there's more to theology than that. We have entered the new world, we are in a new frame of reference,

the horizons have shifted; but we're not in this new environment as a lot of individuals who share an interesting
experience. Somehow or other, in this new world where
new connections are made, the connection between
people is so profound and so unusual that you can't just
reduce it to a group of individuals who happen to be in the
same place. The connection in question is, it seems, a lot
deeper. In this community of the new creation, the new
world, people are depending on one another all the time
at a uniquely important level. The model can be something
of an unwelcome shock. It was in the ancient world, and
the modern world may find it no easier. If you think the
human ideal is being maximally independent, you will
have a serious problem, because if you're a Christian what
you're now involved in is a deep form of dependence on
your neighbours. How does God go on breathing his Spirit
into you, the Spirit of Jesus? He breathes it into you through
the work and witness of the person next to you, as you breathe
it out into them.

In the modern Church, as in the early Church, the person
next to you isn't always the person you would have chosen to
be next to. And you might be surprised by who is breathing
God's Spirit into your life, who is bringing you more fully
alive in God's presence. Once again we are dealing with a set
of new and challenging experiences in which God is being
encountered in unexpected, unprecedented ways; so once
again theology is what begins to happen. St Paul, reflecting
on the plurality and untidiness of the communities that are
springing up, is driven to conclude that what is happening
in these assemblies (the Greek word we translate as 'church'

If you think the human ideal is being maximally independent, you will have a serious problem, because if you're a Christian what you're now involved in is a deep form of dependence on your neighbours.

originally meant something like a convocation, a group of people summoned to debate together or work together) must be more than the gathering together of like-minded individuals, members of a kind of religious society. Paul uses the analogy of the different bits of the human body. Your body is not a kind of committee composed of representatives of the hands, representatives of the feet, representatives of the stomach, all sitting round a table and discussing issues of common concern. In this situation, one of them might leave, and the discussion would still go on – the authorised representative of the interests of the stomach could get up and leave the table while the hands and feet go on negotiating. This is not how any real living organism works.

To paraphrase Paul a little, when I've got a cold, *I've* got a cold – it's not just my nose that has the cold. When I have a heart attack, *I* have a heart attack – it's not just a single organ in my chest that's affected. In the body, everything affects everything; and this is why membership in the Christian community is not just like being part of a group that might go on working even if someone goes off on their own. If bits of your body start disappearing or ceasing to function, you will notice quite soon. If, as Paul puts it, one bit of the body says, 'I can get along perfectly well without the others,' the mistake becomes obvious in short order.

How do Christians think about their life together? How do they think about the way in which the gifts of the Holy Spirit bind them together in dependence on each other? These too are questions for theology. In engaging with them, we begin to understand the pattern of giving and receiving in the flow of the Spirit's work, like the circulation of the blood. We recognise what Paul, at the end of his second letter to the Christians at Corinth, calls the 'communion' or 'fellowship' of the Holy Spirit. It's a very strong word in Greek (*koinonia*) – the 'in-commonness', the togetherness of mutual involvement, that the Spirit gives.

Our theology of what and who Jesus is and about how the Spirit works thus takes us forward to our understanding of the Church – not primarily as an institution, but as the togetherness of people giving and receiving new life. Say the word 'church' and, however hard we try, images come to mind of spires and stained glass, not to mention, alas, anxious or censorious people. We badly need to recover the sense of a new experience of shared life that prompts the use of what was then an unusual word. Paul was looking for a word you might use for an assembly of people invited to come together to take responsibility for each other's lives, so he picked a term often applied to public assemblies of citizens in Roman cities. Now, however, it could be used not just for people working out common policies and regulations, but for those who genuinely depended on one another for their ability to live out in their own lives the effects of God's generosity in sharing love and the freedom that comes from that.

And following on from this, it is quite important to see how Paul approaches the whole business of Christian morality from this starting point. He never seems to think that you can talk about Christian behaviour just in terms of rules sent down from heaven. He wants us to think about what a life looks like when the basic reality is mutual giving and receiving, the building up in one another of a deepened freedom to listen to God and work with the grain of God's nature and purpose. All that he has to say about justice and generosity, about faithfulness in marriage, about the care of those who are forgotten and deprived, about the need constantly to resist temptations to faction and party spirit and aggressive rhetoric towards one another, and much more besides – all of these have to do with what it means to be bound together in this organic way, as a body in which all parts share in the life of the whole. Morality is really a matter of working out what it means to live as a church, as a true body. It's not that some distinct entity called 'the Church' tells us what to do. Rather, it's up to the people who make up the Church to work out what behaviours do and don't show the kind of community a church really is.

There will be a bit more about that in the final chapter; but for now, a further brief word about two things that are central to this working out of what the life of the Church really is. These are the two most significant actions among what we call the sacraments: baptism and Holy Communion.

Sacraments: baptism and Holy Communion

All Christian public worship expresses, first of all, gratitude that God has given his Spirit so that people can live by the power and love of Jesus the Anointed King (which is what 'Christ' means). Admission to a full share in this worship is by baptism – a word that originally meant simply being dipped in water. According to Christian teaching, when water is poured over someone in the name of the Father, the Son and the Holy Spirit, their old life comes to an end – the life of slavery to self, fear, rivalry and delusion – and the new life of the Spirit begins. In the early years of the Christian community, those being baptised would be adults who had accepted belief in Jesus. As the Christian community grew and spread, and families brought up their children to believe, it became more common for children to be baptised. In many churches, there is another ceremony performed by a bishop, confirmation, which is believed to complete, or seal, what baptism does – though there are some differences of opinion as to what exactly this might mean.

Practically all Christian communities meet for the ritual meal of bread and wine called Holy Communion, and sometimes referred to as the Eucharist (from the Greek for thanksgiving) or Mass (from the Latin for sending someone out to do their work). Many churches do this every day, most of them at least once a week. The ceremony has its origins in the action of Jesus the night before his arrest and execution, when he shared a last meal with his disciples. As he said the blessing over the bread and wine at the table, he declared they were his body and blood.

This language has often seemed strange or shocking. But its meaning must be looked for in the context of the Bible as a whole. The prophets of ancient Israel performed symbolic acts to show that God was about to do certain things. So Jesus, as he breaks the bread and shares the wine at supper is performing a prophetic action: the bread broken and eaten shows what will happen to his body in his suffering, and the wine poured out represents his blood shed. And in this suffering of his, God will be acting to free human beings from their slavery and renewing his covenant with his people, his promise always to be present with them. What Jesus achieves in his suffering and dying will therefore be food and drink for his friends, the nourishment that brings life and strength. So when they bless bread and wine in his name, remembering his prophetic action at his last meal, the sharing of this food and drink will be a means for God's new life to enter into them afresh, and for them to become aware of God's faithfulness to his promises. Just as Jesus' human flesh and blood is the place where God's power and Spirit are at work, so in this bread and wine, blessed in his memory, the same power and Spirit are active and present. This bread and wine are alive with divine life and gift just as the flesh and blood of Jesus were in Jerusalem on that night at supper.

But around this central idea many other images and concepts gather. The meal comes to be seen as a Christian version of the Passover meal of the Jews, in which they remember how God led them out of slavery in Egypt and share in eating a lamb. It is like the meal after a sacrifice in which something has been offered to God in order to restore fellowship between God and humanity. It is like the meals Jesus shared with sinners and outcasts to show them that God was ready to welcome and forgive them. And it is like the meals described in the Gospels of Luke and John that Jesus shared with his disciples after he had been raised from death.

It is also the place where prayers are offered for all who need prayer. Because the Christian at Holy Communion

Just as Jesus' human flesh and blood is the place where God's power and Spirit are at work, so in this bread and wine, blessed in his memory, the same power and Spirit are active and present.

stands especially close to Jesus, it is a time to bring our prayers into his prayer. Many Christians say that being at Holy Communion is how we are present in heaven while still being on earth – because we are at our closest to Jesus, praying with his voice, receiving his life. Many of the prayers used all over the Christian world talk about how at the communion service we praise God alongside the angels and all the holy people of the past. When the community meets for communion, it announces that it is one with the whole assembly of God's people, living and dead, on earth and in heaven.

5

Why Scripture?

In the last couple of chapters, I've spent some time describing what I think is going on in the pages of the New Testament. Behind those pages stand the lives of communities across a thousand years or more living around the eastern Mediterranean, communities like those first generations asking what was happening on the day of Pentecost and afterwards, often bewildered and amazed. They have been overtaken by something, dropped down in a new environment, and they are struggling to get their bearings. Every single writer of the New Testament, in their own way, is trying to help people get their bearings. Paul is the most eloquent and copious of them, John perhaps the most profound. But it's just as true of the gospel writers Matthew, Mark and Luke, telling the story of Jesus in such a way as to provide us with the clues and the trails that make the connections for us – connections with the history of the Jewish people, connections with our experience now, connections with others who are reading or have been reading the same text. This exploring of connection, as we'll see, is in fact central to all the biblical writers, whether in Hebrew Scripture (the Old Testament) or Christian Scripture (the New Testament).

It may help to outline a bit of history to start with – something about the first generations of Christians in the decades when and just after the books of Christian Scripture were being written. By the end of the first Christian century, there was the start of a pattern of regular quotation from certain books. It seems as though there was the beginning of a consensus about several works, an agreement that they could be read as reliable sources for thinking about and praying to God. As yet, there was no cast-iron definition of what was in and what was out. As we're often reminded by would-be sensationalist journalists, there were early Christian books that did not make it into the Bible we know, and the boundaries were not set in stone. There was no single authoritative list of contents for Christian Scripture; nor of course was there yet a creed of the kind that developed later. But you had what could be called a set of signals by which Christians could recognise one another, a vocabulary in common. Probably no individual at the end of the first Christian century possessed a Bible: you would have needed a substantial packing case for a very large number of scrolls, and they would have cost an enormous amount. Little black volumes to slip into your pocket were a thing of the distant future. Just as with Jewish Scripture – which was itself going through the last stages of being finalised as a collection at much the same period – a local community might have managed to put together a significant collection of material to be used in public worship. And if you travelled, or met somebody who came from another community in another city, you'd want to know you spoke the same language – about prayer to God as Father, for example, or about the distribution of the gifts of the Holy Spirit in the community, or about the life of believers in Jesus as new creations or a new people.

What the surviving literature and the archaeological evidence point to is a respectable level of convergence at this stage, with Matthew's Gospel especially and several of Paul's letters finding a pretty widespread public.

But as the second Christian century got under way, things became a little more complicated. Some communities and individuals wanted to hold on to a wider range of books, especially of a more speculative kind – what is usually called gnostic literature because of its emphasis on knowledge (*gnosis*) for an elite. Others wanted to narrow the focus because they were concerned about tensions or contradictions between Hebrew and Christian Scripture. They proposed abandoning the Old Testament and regarding the God of Hebrew Scripture as an inferior or even malicious spirit. People had already noticed the problems that some critics of Jewish-Christian religion still like to stress – that the God of Hebrew Scripture sometimes seems to be harsh or cruel or unjust. The difficulty with this neat and disastrous proposal was that Christian Scripture contains a great deal of reference to Jewish Scripture. So unless you are willing to do some very drastic surgery on parts of Christian Scripture as well – and some did not shrink from this solution – you still have to face the tensions. And if you go on editing for acceptability, you might end up with very little indeed. This might be just the bits that don't create problems for you; others, of course, would have different views of what is difficult. The rest of the Church looked at these kinds of solutions and reacted by saying, 'That can't be right. Granted, the Old Testament may pose some problems for us, but this means we simply have to work at it and see if we can map out a consistent pattern beneath the apparent contradictions. What we don't do is take the short cut of just amputating sections to suit ourselves.'

This was part of the process by which the Bible as we know it began to come together – a selective group of early writings by Christians, mostly letters and accounts of the life of Jesus, and the complete authoritative collection of Jewish Scripture as agreed by the rabbis of the first and second Christian centuries. It's tempting to think, when we reflect on the inspiration and authority of Scripture, that there was some sort of original edition; but what we have is the result of a quite lengthy process, not fully settled until the fourth century. Christians, like the Jews before them, came to recognise the Bible as an expression of the essential core of the story they told and the kind of life they had to lead. By the end of the second Christian century, the boundaries were already fairly clear and it was possible to speak of a 'canon' of Scripture. A canon literally means 'a rule, an authoritative standard'. So the biblical canon consisted of the books that could be relied on and needed to be read, heard and followed if the Christian community was to be at peace, living in a harmonious way.

The claim was that these were the books that belonged with Christian identity and that mediated for the readers what God wanted to communicate. Other things on the market, the sort of texts that are still sometimes found in the sands of Egypt or in long-neglected libraries, could safely be ignored. Indeed, not ignoring them could be unsafe as they presented a style of life and teaching regarded as incompatible with the texts that had emerged as central. What was becoming the mainstream

Christian network believed as a very general rule that texts reliably associated with the first generation of apostles had a claim to be taken seriously. When other writings appeared, such as gospels ascribed to Philip or Thomas, there was an appeal to the continuity of use. There was evidence, so it was claimed, that the books favoured by the mainstream networks had been steadily used in public worship and teaching for as far back as memory went, and so had shaped the speech and imagery that helped individuals and communities to become more fully recognisable to each other. The rest might have looked attractively exotic or interesting, it might have looked less weighed down with tensions, but these works failed generations of faithful people, and failed to provide a reliable common point of appeal for diverse local congregations.

As you can see, all this was a fairly rule-of-thumb argument, based on a slow process of sorting and joining up, rather than an instant and comprehensive solution. But that is in itself quite a significant clue about how to read and understand the books of the Bible. Scripture records a process of God taking time with human beings, in a cumulative story of breakthroughs, setbacks, continuity and discontinuity, with texts and narratives that are regularly being reworked and reimagined as the sheer scale of what is being shown about the nature of the limitless God becomes clearer.

Why do Christians treasure the whole Bible?

We have already noted that as well as the writings of the first generation of believers in Jesus, the Christian

Scripture records a process of God taking time with human beings, in a cumulative story of breakthroughs, setbacks, continuity and discontinuity, with texts and narratives that are regularly being reworked and reimagined as the sheer scale of what is being shown about the nature of the limitless God becomes clearer.

Bible contains the Scriptures of the Jewish people. When Christians open it, they do so in order to hear a fuller story of how God's revealing power has been at work in history. God's first actions to free human beings from the effects of the deep failure that took place at the very start of human history are to be seen in God's calling to Noah to re-establish the harmony of the human race and the created order after the catastrophe of the Flood. This was followed by God's calling to Abraham to be the ancestor of a people who would be close to God, who would display the justice and mercy of God and be aligned with God's purposes. This people would later be rescued by God from slavery in Egypt and, through the leadership of Moses, receive a system of law that allowed God's justice and mercy to shape the life of a whole community. Later still, this people would experience a long history of both God's favour and God's judgement, political glory and abject defeat and exile, but would never be abandoned by him. And the Christian conclusion to the whole narrative is that at last God displayed the total and unconditional character of his promise-keeping faithfulness in the life of Jesus as his Word, his gift, his action and presence in the world, so as to gather a people who would this time be not just one national community, but a community of 'every tribe, people and language', as the New Testament says.

The books contained in the Bible are of very diverse character. Unlike the Qur'an, this is not a text delivered in a brief space of time to one person. The Bible is a book that speaks with one voice about God and his will and nature, but it does so – to use a popular Christian image – like a symphony of different voices and instruments of music. It is miraculously held together in one story and one message about God, a story whose climax for Christians is Jesus. Sometimes parts of the Bible are hard to understand; sometimes different passages seem to contradict each other. This is not surprising when you remember that the books of the Bible were written over a period of more than a thousand years. But every word has been discussed and thought about for another two thousand years, and Christians have found that there is always a deep unity of thought, once it is agreed that the life of Jesus is the centre of the picture and that it makes sense of all the rest.

It needs to be added that Christians have all too often spoken as though the books of Hebrew Scripture are important only as a preparation for something more important. This has been one of the strands in the terrible history of Christian antisemitism, and the disgraceful language applied to Jews as representing something over and done with, something that is dead and valueless in itself. It is salutary for Christians – and others – to do some patient study of what Jews themselves say about their Scriptures, and to realise that their interpretation of the texts is a creative and continuing tradition. It is essential for Christians to remember that all they say in relation to Jesus makes sense only against the deep background of his Jewish identity. They are doing just what the Jewish writers and interpreters of Scripture have always done – reworking and reimagining what they have received so as to bring out new depths of meaning. In this light, the relation between Jews and Christians is not that of an outmoded and imperfect faith to a fully up-to-date system. It is that of inseparably related communities doing radically different things with the same core traditions. The differences are indeed profound, and it is not possible to see how within our history they could simply come together in a single vision. But it is right to pray for a coming together – of a kind God alone could know – and to be ready to learn from Judaism as a living reality, not a museum piece.

Looking very briefly at the content of our Bibles, we begin with the group called the Torah ('the Law') by Jews, or the Pentateuch (the 'Five Books') in Greek. These books describe the creation, the Flood, the history of Abraham and his family, the rescue of the people of Israel from Egypt and the giving of the law to Moses. Then come books of historical chronicles taking us up to the great disaster of the deportation of large numbers of the Jewish people to Babylon after a traumatic invasion and defeat. There are books of hymns and proverbial wisdom, and the messages of the prophets, who declared God's judgement against the people's failures in justice and integrity, and promised that God would restore them if they turned to him. We also have a couple of books about how the people of Israel came back from their exile in Babylon, as well as a few vivid stories of individuals (notably women like Ruth and Esther) who have a key role in the history of God's people. And there is one unique and revolutionary book (Job), attempting to think through the problem of innocent suffering.

Turning to Christian Scripture, we have the four Gospels ('gospel' means 'a declaration of good news'), which tell the story of Jesus. These are followed by the Acts of the Apostles, summarising the spread of the faith and introducing us to the most energetic Christian communicator of that generation, Paul of Tarsus. Then there is a collection of letters (epistles) ascribed to Paul, Peter, John, James and Jude, writings that give guidance on matters of belief and behaviour to different Christian communities. To conclude, there is the Revelation to John, a chaotically vivid vision of the last days of the world, and the coming of Jesus in glory to judge all people.

Christians believe that the whole Bible is inspired by God – that is, they believe that the texts that make up the Bible were composed with the help of the Holy Spirit – and that, taken all together and read in the context of prayer and worship, they communicate what God wants us to know. Some Christians (most Christians in the past, many in the present) believe that this means the Bible is never wrong about any statement of fact. Others, while agreeing that the Bible is the final authority, would say that this rather misunderstands the point of the Bible. They would maintain that the point is not to give us infallible information about all sorts of things, but to provide a reliable guide to what God is like and how he works, and what this means for our own lives and well-being in reconciled relationship with God. In this latter framework, it is possible to say that the Bible does not need to be correct about every single matter of fact. Witnesses to everyday situations may be mistaken about issues such as dates, personal names or stories, geographical details and so on without making their testimony valueless or untrue. We do not need to think that God dictated the Bible to its writers, directly putting vast amounts of information into their minds; rather that he worked with

Christians believe that the whole Bible is inspired by God – that is, they believe that the texts that make up the Bible were composed with the help of the Holy Spirit – and that, taken all together and read in the context of prayer and worship, they communicate what God wants us to know.

and in their human minds to communicate his purpose, to tell us what we need to know in order to be set free from our mistakes and sins.

Christians have spent much energy on the study of the Bible's texts and how they came to be composed. They have established the best evidence for the texts and have discovered and discussed very early examples of the manuscripts (we have a part of John's Gospel on a piece of parchment dated less than a hundred years after Jesus). Sometimes the results of this study have been seen as disturbing by those who insist upon the accuracy of every detail. But a large number of Christians accept the results of scholarly study as confirming the idea that the Bible tells one story in several different voices.

As the pattern of the whole story suggests, the New Testament, written by Jesus' first followers and friends, cannot be understood without the Old Testament. Jesus works to recreate the people of God, just as the ancient prophets of Israel did; but he extends the boundaries of the people of God to include all nations. The God who once made a covenant, an alliance, with the people of Israel now makes a covenant with all who trust in God because of what Jesus says and does.

6

Why tradition?

The issues that have kept coming up since the early centuries of the Church, as we have seen, are regularly questions about the limits and criteria of what you can say about Jesus and his community. They concern what your sources are for saying what you do, how what you say about various subjects joins up, what your authority is for claiming to be talking truth and sense. They are about the boundaries and truth conditions for Christian thinking; about what has come to be called orthodoxy, right teaching. Why might this matter? What is involved here? And aren't there enormous risks in tying down something both very mysterious and very personal?

I want to suggest a general answer to this and then address some more particular issues. The general answer is in line with what I have been trying to sketch so far. Somewhere in the background of all this is the question of what we need to do when we are trying to talk about God, in order to keep open the enormous breadth and scope of what the New Testament says about Jesus and the Spirit. This is the most basic criterion. Are we saying less than the Bible wants to say about Jesus and the Spirit? Because, as we've seen, the language of Christian Scripture is trying to push the boundaries again and again, so as to say as much as can possibly be said about the real, comprehensive newness of the new world that God has created through Jesus. A great deal of controversy in the early Church, and indeed later on, comes down to the challenge of whether we are trying to shrink those boundaries again. Are we drawing in our horns a bit, risking saying less than the New Testament says?

In the often seriously complicated controversies of the third, fourth and fifth centuries of the Church, this was the underlying worry; and perhaps this helps to explain a little why passions were aroused over what may seem to us at first sight relatively minor points of detail. The question is consistently, 'Does this or that way of speaking do justice to the scale of the claim made by the Bible and indeed by the regular language of worship?' If we must have a definition of heresy as the early Church understood it, maybe the most useful one is that heresy was seen as saying less about God than the God who had acted in Jesus and the Spirit deserved.

It's always been taken for granted, right from the start, that adequate, fitting language for God has to take its cue from the Bible. The people who started working on theological issues in the earliest Church didn't think that the Bible simply answered all your questions instantly – in today's terms, as if it were a sort of spiritual agony aunt, or even a computer program where you just put in your question and out comes a neat answer. They knew that the Bible was quite a puzzling set of writings, and that you had to make the connections; and making the connections meant that you had to pray and work and think very hard.

For a very long time, 'doing theology' was really a name for Bible study at a certain level of professionalism.

If we must have a definition of heresy as the early Church understood it, maybe the most useful one is that heresy was seen as saying less about God than the God who had acted in Jesus and the Spirit deserved.

Even in the Middle Ages, when people were beginning to do much more advanced and abstract philosophical reflection on Christian teaching, the greatest theologian of the period, St Thomas Aquinas in the thirteenth century, assumed from the outset that of course theology was studying Scripture. As he puts it, using the Latin terms, *sacra doctrina* (holy teaching) is *sacra scriptura* (holy Scripture), studying the holy writings. At root, he says, it is all about thinking through the lives of the people we meet in Scripture, 'the persons through whom revelation reaches us', clarifying how it is that they show God to us. When faced with working through several thousand words of Thomas Aquinas's philosophical speculations, you might be forgiven for thinking, 'What exactly has this got to do with Abraham or Moses?' But this really is what he believed he was doing. It might take a very long time to get to this degree of abstraction and complication from the stories of Abraham or Moses, but St Thomas was convinced that, at the end of the day, we are just trying to work out what these lives, these stories in the Bible, are showing us about God. That is the essence of holy teaching, of theology.

What about the Reformation?

At the time of the Reformation, the question of how to do theology became a bit more challenging and controversial. The elaborate structures of thinking and behaving that had grown up through the centuries seemed very far from where things began in the Bible; and as more people learned to read and the scriptural texts were translated into more languages, more and more readers began to challenge interpretations that had become customary. The question 'Where exactly do you find that in the Bible?' became a common challenge, and provoked bitter controversy. At one extreme, Christians were saying that unless something was there in so many words in the Bible, it should be rejected. At the other extreme, defenders of the status quo insisted that the tradition of the Church was a reliable source of truth and that there were unwritten teachings that had been preserved by the Church even though they were not in the biblical text. Most serious thinkers at the time, whether Catholic or Protestant, stood somewhere between these points, but the climate of the time certainly encouraged unhelpful oppositions – and we are still living with the consequences of this.

The leading theologians who were arguing for far-reaching reforms in the Church were in fact pretty clear that while the Bible had to be 'set free' to prompt awkward questions about what had developed over the centuries, this did not mean that you could just read the text as an individual, as if no one else was reading it or had ever read it before. They were in no doubt that – as we noted in the last chapter – you are always reading the Bible 'in company'. And so, to be a theologian, you need to read the people who have read the Bible, however much you want to underline the primary importance of the Bible. A really great reforming advocate like John Calvin brings to bear a wide range of scholarship as he reads the Bible, drawing on the best of the early Church and the Middle Ages – not uncritically, but always with a readiness to learn from what has gone before. And this is where we see something of the real meaning of tradition in the life of the Church. Tradition is not just what we happen to have inherited – that will always need to be probed and tested in the light of the basic themes of the Bible. The tradition we must respect is the ongoing process of paying attention to people who have read the Bible before us.

So we don't treat tradition as if it were something alongside the Bible and comparable to it. It is the record of other people reading it, and not in itself revelation. But in an important sense neither is the Bible really revelation when looked at absolutely on its own, without any context. Those who try to treat it in this way notoriously get tangled up in all kinds of contradictions and absurdities. As we read, we need all the help we can get, so it is a good idea to invite a lot of people to share the process as we read – the people who have read it before us, and the people who are reading it now in different contexts. The importance of this has become even greater as we Europeans and North Americans realise just how narrow much of our reading has been, and how shamefully it has been biased towards what suits us (think of those hundreds of years when Western Christians of all sorts genuinely believed that the Bibe was compatible with the slave trade . . .).

Sometimes we talk as though the Reformation were a great moment of breakthrough in the direction of individualism, allowing everyone to take the Bible off to their own private room and work out its meaning in isolation. On the contrary: the great Reformers believed that it was important to have the Bible in people's everyday language precisely so that they could read it together. It wasn't so that they could shut

themselves up in their attic and work out the date of the end
of the world from some baffling chapter in the Revelation
to John. This is how quite a lot of Christian sects have got
started. For the great Reformers, the Bible was a book you
read together, inviting people from the past as well as the
present into the room with you, and listening prayerfully for
wisdom in reading that may be deeper than yours or than
what seems to make sense to people just like you.

This is the 'Catholic' element that the first Protestants still
held on to in the early decades of the Reformation; and the
Catholics of that era themselves took seriously the challenge
to think through more carefully the inherited formulae and
practices, and put great resources into better texts of the
Bible and better histories of the Church. Against some of
the thinking of the later Middle Ages, which had made it so
hard to raise any critical questions, the theologians on both
sides of the Reformation agreed that there had to be harder
and more critical work to understand what had been passed
down over the centuries. Hardly anyone disagreed that the
Bible came first. But they recognised the risk of suggesting
that it would simply give you a short cut to crystal-clear
answers for every issue that might come up – theological,
historical or moral. Against this they said, in effect, 'No, be
hospitable in your reading. Welcome the great readers of the
past to read with you.'

That is still extremely good advice – to read the Bible with
the great readers of the Bible, the holy and wise people who
have read it before us. They were not always right, any more
than we and our contemporaries are. Sometimes, just like
us, they read badly and clumsily, or even got it completely,

disastrously wrong. Think of a giant like St Augustine in the fourth and fifth centuries. He was undoubtedly the most brilliant, passionate, profound, enriching theologian of the early Church, perhaps in the whole history of the Church. Reading Augustine is likely to excite and stir you to the core – his account of his journey to full faith as an adult, his meditations on the Trinity, his sermons on the Psalms or the Gospels, his extraordinary analysis of what the gospel means for human society . . . And then perhaps you turn to some of what he wrote about the punishment that awaits children born in original sin, or about the arbitrary character of God's choice of who is to receive grace and who isn't, and you're likely to feel bewildered that so great and generous a mind could come up with such jarring ideas. But one advantage of reading in company is that you can't avoid the recognition that even the wisest and best are not infallible. And the good news is that Christians don't have to be infallible; they just have to be prepared to learn and to be penitent. In fact, St Augustine devoted a whole work late in life to explaining where he thought he had got things wrong: a book called *Retractations*, which takes us right through all the things he said in his career as a theologian. What an extraordinary example that a man of his intellectual stature and holiness was able to say, 'I thought I was right, but I wasn't.'

Scripture and tradition are not two things on the same level. Tradition is part of the ongoing process of reading Scripture. If we take tradition away from this context, what we are likely to be left with is traditionalism, which is not especially good for us, as it pushes us towards nostalgia, the desire just to repeat the way things have been. But tradition

Scripture and tradition are not two things on the same level. Tradition is part of the ongoing process of reading Scripture. If we take tradition away from this context, what we are likely to be left with is traditionalism, which is not especially good for us.

as the living reading of the Bible in company with as many people as possible is something different. One modern theologian of the Eastern Orthodox Church described tradition as 'the charismatic memory of the Church'. This is a wonderful phrase. Tradition is what we remember, but what we remember in and through the gift of Jesus' Spirit, which gives us the sense and critical discernment both to receive gratefully and to go on learning and not repeating things for the sake of it – let alone repeating deeply entrenched mistakes.

It is interesting that many reform movements in the Church – from the Reformation itself to the campaign to abolish slavery to the various modern movements to balance a very unbalanced history of Christian attitudes to women – include an element of going back; of interrogating our collective memory and asking, 'Did we hear this correctly?' Tradition, properly understood, allows us to re-read the Bible constantly, because it shows us how the Bible has always been re-read. Not to conform it to whatever happens to be fashionable, but to keep asking whether we have yet fully grasped the way in which the Bible hangs together, makes a coherent whole. And this is yet again about an orthodoxy that seeks to say no less about God than he has revealed – a long task, but one in which God's grace accompanies us.

7

Why reason?

In making sense of it all, Christians have very often wanted to add another element to the summary of how we do theology: not only Scripture and tradition, but reason as well. Some have called it the third leg of the stool, and it is a triad especially popular with Anglicans. But the word 'reason' is not the easiest to understand, especially as it can suggest to us something like purely logical argument.

In an older context, though, it means a good deal more than this. We all have ways of making sense of our world through the tools that our culture offers us. People's minds work in particular ways in different historical environments, and we can't simply transfer every category of one period or context or language into another. We are always, literally or metaphorically, translating. And when we come to reading the Bible, we need translation in all sorts of ways; we don't simply step right out of our ordinary habits of thinking and turn into completely different people. We bring the best of our habits of thinking and our disciplines of thinking to making sense of the Bible.

As with tradition, it's not as if reason is another source of revelation alongside the text of Scripture. Tradition is the deposit of a long process of reading the Bible; reason is the equipment we bring to that reading today. The central fact remains what the Bible witnesses to. Tradition is reading it in

We all have ways of making sense of our world through the tools that our culture offers us. People's minds work in particular ways in different historical environments, and we can't simply transfer every category of one period or context or language into another.

company with others through the centuries; reason is reading it using our common sense and making the best of what is around us in our environment to bring the record alive today.

To clarify further, this is not to suggest that what the biblical texts – or the traditional creeds – have to say is radically foreign to how we think now, or that what seemed to be truth in another era isn't true now. It is not to adopt a wholesale relativism, in which truth is reduced to what we happen to be able to make sense of today. It is simply to say that new and different perspectives open up in the human world and inevitably modify how we read any text from the past. Any modern performance of Shakespeare's *Hamlet* can't avoid the fact that we are aware of more psychological layers in the relationships between children and parents than anyone in 1600 could have articulated. But it's not that Shakespeare didn't know at some level how this worked, just by being the artist he was; our words are different, and that difference itself opens up new insights. We do not write off or patronise a genius of the past, but work at understanding how what such a genius thought they were doing feeds into our framework of understanding. That modern framework is challenged and changed, just as the surface patterns of the historical text are challenged by our questioning. Something emerges that is neither the (impossible) re-presentation of a lost world nor the statement of an equally impossible purely contemporary set of ideas. After all, we are able to think what we now think only because others have thought before us. So bringing reason to bear on the text of Scripture as part of doing theology is not exposing traditional belief to the hostile light of some imagined pure modern rationality;

it is deploying as best we can the rich resources of the mind and imagination as they have developed.

People become anxious about reason because many do still nurture the strange myth of an absolute and disembodied rationality. This is the kind of thing many came to believe as a result of the European Enlightenment, for which certain things, certain styles of proof and argument, are self-evidently true, quite independently of how they are learned and tested in the entire complexity of human life. And this includes feelings as well as thought, and often works through trust, practical experience and a whole range of informal ways of arriving at what we think is reliable knowledge. There have been strands of theology that take for granted a post-Enlightenment model of reasoning. These pose fundamental challenges to a lot of the doctrinal settlements of an earlier age, arguing that our modern minds need to rethink – or even abandon – biblical or historical formulations of faith. It is emphatically not wrong or somehow blasphemous to note where older texts are assuming models of the world that are not ours, where expanded knowledge of history, geography or human physiology makes it impossible just to repeat older formulations as though nothing has changed. But if we are still reading in the company of those who have gone before us, we are bound to be listening as well as speaking, asking what they knew that we don't, as well as the other way around; recognising that there will be ways of hearing and seeing what they saw and heard, even if we need to do some hard work decoding the structures of thinking they used.

It is not as though our contemporary reasoning is just working on a set of phenomena out there, using timelessly valid methods. In theology, we are reasoning with those who share the organic life that is the Church, reasoning with the grain of what Christians are already saying, praying and singing. There was a fashion – very powerful and prevalent in the theology of the middle of the last century – for concluding that the classical doctrines of the Trinity or the divinity of Christ were incapable of rational proof, or based on insufficient evidence, or dependent on outdated or impossible philosophical assumptions. This was rooted in a faulty sense of how thinking itself works, as if it were always about bringing our intellectual powers to bear on a set of neutral facts 'out there'. The truth is that I am already inside the world that the doctrines represent. It is where I live, and it is rather odd to try to rebuild the roof over my head.

Reasoning – and it may be more helpful to use that word rather than 'reason' if the latter suggests some abstract universal power – is bound to be part of how Christians converse with what they receive as members of the ongoing, continuous reality of the Church. And in this conversation, Christians will naturally bring to bear the agenda of their culture as they read and listen. But this should never be uncritically, never just insisting on what society takes for granted. It should be with an honest willingness to have our minds enlarged both by what we read in Scripture and tradition and by what our own culture suggests as good questions to ask. We might come to a reasoned conclusion that what seems to be the plain meaning of a text in Scripture or a traditional phrase in worship is actually capable of nuance, so that its essential importance is seen to be something slightly different from what we first thought. This is the process that, for example, has led Christians to think through biblical prohibitions against lending money for interest; to modify the apparent absolutism of Jesus' sayings about divorce; to put in context Paul's injunctions about how women behave in church; and, most controversially in recent decades, to open up questions around same-sex relationships. The argument is not between those who are faithful to Scripture and those who are in bondage to the spirit of the age, but between people applying different kinds and levels of reasoned interpretation to what is in front of them. Even the most dedicated traditionalist is in fact using principles of reasoning that are meant to be recognisable – not just repeating what is on the page. And probing the text to look for deeper levels of consistency that might take us beyond what looks immediately obvious is not at all the same as the buccaneering enthusiasm for rewriting or editing out anything that we find odd or offensive.

Historically, these elements of Scripture, tradition and reason have been the touchstones for what we say theologically. We can and must be asking: am I saying something that tries to say less than there is in the Bible? Am I reading all this in company with the holiest and wisest readers of the Bible across the ages? Am I using my common sense, and taking seriously the contemporary resources that have shaped my mind and imagination? Doing theology responsibly involves dealing with all those questions as honestly as possible; and the greatest theologians of the modern era at their best show how some of this responsibility plays out.

Theology in action

To take just one of these formidable figures, let me mention Karl Barth, a great Swiss Reformed theologian, probably the foremost Protestant thinker of the twentieth century. He was always crystal clear that what he was doing as a theologian was simply reading the Bible. There is an anecdote about him as an old man being asked by a journalist to summarise his thinking in a single sentence. Barth, author of some millions of words in his dozens of books, replied: 'Jesus loves me, this I know, for the Bible tells me so.' His magisterial multi-volume work on church dogmatics includes long passages of detailed wrestling with biblical interpretation; and he repeatedly turns back to the great theologians of the past, from the early Church to the Reformation and beyond, to enrich and reinforce his argument.

But there is more to his work than one might gather immediately from the writing alone. He was doing his theology at the time of the rise to power of the Nazis in Germany. For him, the question of what was different about the Church was an immediate one, as Hitler's government sought to control the German churches and force the exclusion from the churches of anyone with Jewish ancestry. Barth was an unequivocal opponent of the Nazi regime. In 1935, he was instrumental in drafting the strongest statement of resistance to the state's racial policies that had yet appeared from Christian sources, declaring that any criterion for belonging in the Church other than faith in Christ was a rejection of God's authority. As a result of his political activities, he had to leave his position in Germany and return to his native Switzerland. In effect, Barth was saying that we can never take what our society is telling us as a criterion for theology; theology arises from reflecting on what the Church is, and so ultimately reflecting on who Christ is. It can't be reduced to vaguely religious musings on the existing social order, because its own social order is not defined by the prevailing culture. It is a social order in which the mutual gift of life between believers, through God's Spirit and power, mandates a degree of justice and equality that goes beyond just trying to make unfair systems work a bit better.

Barth was by no means always clear about what this might mean. Notoriously, despite his own fierce opposition to the application of racial laws in the Church, he did not give priority to denouncing the atrocities directed against the Jews as a whole community that were already well under way in the 1930s, and his own work is shadowed in several ways by the long legacy of Christian antisemitism. But the principle was not in doubt that the theologian had to be ready to test the agenda any society was providing against the fact of the community that had been created by God's invitation and gift. This, you could say, is how Barth applied reason in his theology. He read Scripture and asked how the questions that lay behind the biblical text came into practical focus in the immediate context – questions like: what kind of community is it that happens when God is at work? What sort of actions or policies build up such a community and what sort of actions destroy it?

Right up to the end of his life, Barth continued to work in this way. In the 1950s, as the Cold War settled in as a

Theology arises from reflecting on what the Church is, and so ultimately reflecting on who Christ is. It can't be reduced to vaguely religious musings on the existing social order, because its own social order is not defined by the prevailing culture.

fact of global life, he was writing some very challenging and sophisticated material about nuclear weapons. He believed that the possession of nuclear weapons was completely incompatible with Christian faith, and that opposition to nuclear warfare was as serious a test of Christian integrity as the racial laws of the Third Reich.

These elements of his later theology are not all that well known, unfortunately, but here as much as in the 1930s we can see him confronting the assumptions of his society, doing a theology in which what is central is always the question of what makes the Church different. His deeply theological approach to such issues will not win everyone's approval, no doubt, but the point is that, for him, any counter-argument worth the name would have to begin from the same essentially theological basis, the same question about what sort of community the Church is.

Barth once said that the theologian should work with the Bible in one hand and the newspaper in the other. He would have been the very last person to suggest that they were of equal importance in discovering anything about the nature and action of God, but what he was saying is that the imaginative struggle and exhilaration that lie behind the pages of Scripture are vital in shaping our prayerful and intelligent response to whatever crisis our age presents us with. If we try to do our theology like this, we shall keep alive the kind of critical and helpfully restless perspective that allows us to be free from fashion and convention and unthinking majority opinion. This will make Christians awkward partners in society – and not every issue on which some Christians are moved to take an independent stand will win the agreement of every Christian. But this is what Christian reasoning looks like. It is not an impersonal method that will deliver right answers, not a narrow concern with proof and certainty. It is the skill of testing our society's assumptions and practices – and our own individual taken-for-granted views – against the record of that creative ferment that stands behind the text of the Bible: human minds stretched to find words and ideas that might do justice to a drastically new level of belonging with other humans and with God.

8

Why does it matter?

This final chapter is about what effect the Christian gospel might have on our lives and our world today. Why does it matter what we believe? What difference does it all make?

We saw in Chapter 1 that, in the gospel, faith means we can say that it's possible to see and acknowledge our failure and our recurrent fears with clarity, but also to know that if we want healing, there are no conditions. It's possible to see these things and accept God's invitation to be healed, restored, forgiven and made whole. Stating it like that is in some ways still fairly general, so now I want to think a bit more about the states of mind, the attitudes and values that may flow from a faithful acceptance of such an invitation.

Faith, understood in this way, makes possible at least three things. First of all, faith makes possible realism and perspective. It makes it possible for us to see ourselves with detachment – in the positive sense of that word. We are able to see ourselves not defensively and anxiously, and not vainly and smugly either, but with honesty and hope, sometimes inglorious, sometimes unfaithful, always redeemable.

In the perspective of faith I see myself as somebody who consistently fails but is loved. I see myself as somebody who is called, summoned and entrusted with responsibility for myself, for others, for my society and world, called to make God's generous, just, compassionate action visible in all areas of life; and I see myself as failing repeatedly to live up to this. I see the possibility of restoration and new beginnings, because God is always the same one who invites and gives. At no point in that cycle am I allowed to see myself as an ultimate waste of space. I can see myself realistically; I don't have to pretend I'm better than I am, I don't even have to pretend I'm worse than I am. I have to recognise my limits, my nature as a growing being and as a being that makes mistakes. And if I see myself in this way, this has a major impact on how I see other human beings, allowing me to step back from the prevailing models and myths about conflict, threat and the need to hold on to power so that no one else can challenge or change me.

So, second, this sort of faith makes possible a way of valuing what's around us. If the world really is grounded in some unimaginable act of final unselfishness, then all we encounter is capable of being seen as gift. As we have a secure anchorage in the unbroken loving action of the source of all things, so has everyone and everything else. As we have a share in that eternal gift, so everyone and everything has. We have been given space and time to grow into intimacy with holy love. The person next to us issues from divine giving, the material environment issues from divine giving; nothing is just there. Everything and everyone is given.

Third, then, if all this is true, if indeed all things somehow flow from God's eternal giving, the natural way to live as human beings in the world is in giving and receiving in a mutual intimacy – not only intimacy with holy love at the centre of everything, but intimacy with one another, an intimacy that commits us to making one another more human. We act in ways that release possibilities in one another. You could broaden this still further and speak of the possibility of an intimacy with the whole world around us that both allows the world to make us more human and allows us to make the world more itself. This attitude of respect towards our environment is something that has come to seem so remote for our so-called advanced or developed societies.

Perspective and realism, evaluation of things as gift, a sense that we are called to committed intimacy in making each other more human – these elements that are made possible by the kind of faith we have been trying to explore – provide a very robust ground on which to stand against opposite styles of living that are uncomfortably familiar:

- *Emotional infantilism*: the utter lack of perspective that puts my immediate needs and the gratification of my immediate passions at the centre. This can show itself in manipulative relations, refusal to take responsibility and forgetfulness of the humanity and need of others, and it can equally show itself (as Jesus so often pointed out) in censoriousness and superiority, the refusal to see clearly.
- *Exploitative selfishness*: the desire to draw the whole human and non-human environment into the great hungry stomach of my individual ego, or of the collective ego of a culture or power bloc, or the ultimate collective ego of humanity exploiting the world it inhabits. This is an attitude that ravages and ruins the world around us and lets itself believe that massive structural unfairness, inequality and violence are simply built into the way things are.

• *Calculation and suspicion in human relationships*: the cynical and corrosive outlook that assumes other individuals, other groups, other nations and the world at large are all there to be used as means to our own ends – and that this is also how others see us, so that everything is reduced to winning or losing.

If you don't see these things around in our culture, it may be that you are not looking very hard. All the possibilities opened up by faith have something to do with seeing more fully. As such they open the door to a way of resisting the most deeply destructive elements of the society we're in, the global culture that all of us in one way or another and in varying degrees inhabit. What difference might faith make in relation to the world of politics? Perhaps, above all, faith conceived in this way both helps us diagnose the sickness with greater truthfulness and gives us the capacity and energy to live in a community that is not defined by winning and losing (which is what the Church is supposed to be, believe it or not . . .).

What do you want? Come and see

In this little book I've been trying to say something about the overall character of Christian commitment, a character that is best expressed in terms not only of seeing but also of seeing that we're not seeing everything. I have tried to anchor that a bit in the way in which the basic Christian story is told in the Gospel of John, and to suggest how seeing the world as Jesus invites us to see it in John's Gospel begins to nurture in us a set

All the possibilities opened up by faith have something to do with seeing more fully. As such they open the door to a way of resisting the most deeply destructive elements of the society we're in.

of human responses capable of becoming an effective ground of resistance to what's most destructive in our world.

You might well say that this is all very attractive, but is there any particular reason for thinking that it's true? This is a question that everyone has to answer for themselves, precisely because the perspective offered by John's Gospel is not that of knockdown arguments, but of invitation. We're never going to get to the point where we can say, 'Here is the proof and any fool can see that this is how we should approach reality.' And this is why I mentioned earlier the significance of both science and art in understanding faith. There's an element of risk involved in all our significant commitments. The scientist embarking on a new direction of experimentation is taking risks that will lead to a whole series of non-confirmations of a theory before, finally, perhaps something clicks. But this in turn will set off a new train of questions and risks. Or again, when we're faced with a great work of the imagination – a poem, film, play or novel – it's not as though the author comes to us and says, 'I can prove to you that this is how reality is.' The author is saying something a lot more like Jesus is at the beginning of John's Gospel: 'Come and see. Discover what you can see by standing here with me.' And if by standing here it's possible to see what otherwise I can't see, I may perhaps at least begin to suspect that there is truth to be seen from this perspective, a truth that I could not discover – let alone invent – on my own.

To come out of, say, a production of *King Lear* or a performance of Mozart's 'Requiem' feeling shaken, uncertain and disturbed is not uncommon. I have been brought to see something I had not bargained for, even (sometimes) something I'd rather not have had to cope with. There's more than I had thought, more in the world of human imagination than I'd reckoned with. I have been put in touch with things I might feel more comfortable not knowing, but if I want to be honest about my world, I can't ultimately avoid them. So when the question 'Is all this true?' arises about the Christian faith, part of the answer is that if, by standing where Jesus invites us to stand, we see more than we would otherwise see, if we see a world larger than we thought we inhabited, we must at least ask ourselves: 'Is this not after all a real, a truthful, place to stand?' Perhaps we must also ask: 'Is my hesitation based on being afraid of the larger reality that is opening up?' And if this even might be the truth, if this just might be the grain of the real world, do we really want to hide from it, unmanageable as it may seem?

The story of Jesus as it's presented to us in the Gospel of John, and the rest of the Christian Bible, is unlike any other in that it holds together, inseparably, the twofold vision I've tried to evoke: the overwhelming reality of divine gift, the terrifying reality of human self-deceit and fear. The story of Jesus is not just an epiphany, a revelation of glory and no more; nor is it just a set of instructions dropped down from heaven, or a Very Good Example of human life. It is a manifestation of beauty and terror, landing in our world in the form of a story that challenges our usual default settings as anxious and selfish creatures. It spells out the way in which love dissolves fear.

There are all kinds of experiences, epiphanies, manifestations of the holy. There is a wonderful German poem (by Rilke) about an ancient Greek statue, ending with the memorable lines: 'There is no place where you are unseen.

You have to change your life.' This sense of a revelation that invites you to change is part of what the gospel is about; but it is not quite everything. The revelation is itself a revelation of an act of love realised in the life and death and rising again of Jesus, into which you are invited to come, and with which you are both invited and enabled to co-operate. Come and see. See whether it is possible for you to discover fresh horizons from here and to be made alive in this way.

Across the human world many ways are proposed for human healing, for the restoration of humanity. But the claim of the gospel is quite simply that here, in this encounter with this person, we are brought to what the Gospel of John itself describes as a secure and eternal place, 'in the bosom of the Father', next to the heart of all things, the place where fear becomes meaningless.

So, in considering what Christianity is all about, and what faith in Jesus really means, we are left with a question, and an invitation. 'What do you want?' says Jesus; and then, 'Come and see.' And we might remember those other profoundly resonant words in the Gospels that Jesus speaks to his friends: 'Launch out into the deep.' Understand that your life lies in the not knowing as well as the knowing. Your life lies in understanding your limits, in letting go and allowing love, reconciliation and intimacy to flourish; in aligning yourself with the energy of creative gift that sustains the entire universe. If this begins to hang together as a possible ground for living in this damaged and intermittently wonderful world, we shall have begun to discover what Christian commitment might mean.

In considering what Christianity is all about, and what faith in Jesus really means, we are left with a question, and an invitation. 'What do you want?' says Jesus; and then, 'Come and see.'

Questions for group discussion or personal reflection

Chapter 1: What is faith?

1 Think about the idea of faith as a process of 'education' that's meant to help you see behind surfaces and understand the depth of reality. Where have you identified moments that encourage you to inhabit a larger, more expansive world rather than a limited one? And do those moments connect with your expectation/ experience of religious belief?

2 St John's Gospel puts a paradox before us: recognising your inability to see clearly is the first step towards true vision. How does this idea resonate with your own experiences of self-awareness and growth? What are some of the moments, when facing your limitations and misconceptions, that have led to a deeper understanding or a significant personal transformation?

3 The story of Jesus is a picture of 'glory' – the radiance of selfless love that throws a new light on everything. What challenges does this picture present to your own mental and spiritual habits?

Chapter 2: What is Christianity?

1 Christians understand God as 'Trinity': Father, Son and Holy Spirit, three distinct but completely interwoven centres of activity. How does this help in thinking about God's very nature as love and wisdom – not just having loving and wise characteristics but actually *being* those things?

2 Does thinking about Jesus as the embodiment of divine wisdom and order have an impact on your view of human dignity and purpose?

3 How does the idea that human beings are born into a world already diminished by destructive forces and the confused inheritance of untruthfulness ('original sin') impact your understanding of personal accountability?

4 How does believing in Jesus as the restorer of the life-giving relationship between God and humanity shape how you think about human potential for change and the ability to live in harmony with God's will?

Chapter 3: What is theology?

1 In Acts 19, Paul encounters disciples who had 'not yet received the Holy Spirit'. How do we connect the ritual acknowledgement of faith in baptism (especially perhaps the baptism of babies) and the transformative experience we associate with the Holy Spirit?

2 If you're a Christian believer, where have you most fully sensed in your life the transforming effect of the Spirit's presence and guidance?

3 If theology is the process of 'making Christian sense', connecting life experiences with the story of Jesus, is this something you're aware of doing? What sort of questions come up in this context, and how do you try to understand your place in the world through the lens of faith?

Chapter 4: Why church?

1 If the Christian community is an interdependent body where each member contributes to the whole in mutual giving and receiving, how does this inspire and sustain Christians in their spiritual journey?

2 Do the stories of Jesus' meals with sinners and outcasts deepen your understanding of Jesus meeting for meals with his friends before and after his crucifixion? And does this help in understanding what's going on in Holy Communion?

Chapter 5: Why Scripture?

1 Are your ideas about the authority and inspiration of the Bible affected (positively or negatively) by thinking about the Bible as a set of texts that take shape gradually in the context of a community's life?

2 There is plenty of diversity within the Bible, from historical narratives to Wisdom literature, prophetic writings, letters ... How does this variety contribute to your understanding of God's character and actions in history?

3 What do you think is the relationship between Hebrew and Christian Scripture (the 'Old Testament' and the 'New Testament')? In what ways does Jesus come to be seen as fulfilling and extending the story of God's covenant with humanity?

Chapter 6: Why tradition?

1 The early Church grappled with defining the boundaries of what could be said about Jesus and his community, focusing on maintaining the breadth and scope of the New Testament's message. Why do you think it was important to establish those boundaries?

2 It's important to distinguish between 'tradition' as a living process of interpreting Scripture and 'traditionalism' as just repeating how things were seen and done in the past. How do we balance respect for the insights of previous generations with being open to new interpretations and understandings?

3 There have probably been times when you've had to re-evaluate your beliefs or practices. How did this feel, and how did you cope with the unsettlement of long-treasured perspectives? Has it seemed like a spiritual enrichment or a loss? Or both?

Chapter 7: Why reason?

1 Do you think that your cultural and intellectual context influences the way you read the Bible and your approach

to traditional church teaching? Can we ever get beyond this? Do we need to?

2 Karl Barth's approach to theology involved being very sceptical about the importance of being in tune with current thinking, or being positive about human achievements. He thought this way of thinking had a lot to do with weakening people's resistance to Nazi attempts to control the German churches. How does Barth's insistence on testing social practice against the teaching of the Church challenge what you think about the relationship today between faith and human reason and between the Church and a not very religious society?

Chapter 8: Why does it matter?

1 One way of thinking about Christian faith is to see it as the idea that everything and everyone around us issues from divine giving. How might viewing the world and the people in it as gifts from God influence your attitudes and actions towards them in your daily interactions and environmental consciousness?

2 Christian faith is less about providing a set of cast-iron winning arguments, more about an invitation to 'come and see'. Can you think of times when you have accepted an invitation like that? What sort of changes and challenges did it involve and did it make a lasting difference?

3 We all have moments when we have to confront uncomfortable truths about ourselves and our world.

In your experience, have these moments led to personal growth or deeper understanding? How does the vision of unconditional divine love and divine commitment help dissolve our fear of growing through these tough times?